Annie Besant

THE
LAW OF POPULATION.

ITS CONSEQUENCES

AND

Its Bearing Upon Human Conduct and Morals.

BY

ANNIE BESANT.

THIRTY-FOURTH THOUSAND.

New American Edition from the Thirty-fifth Thousand, English Edition.

FAIR PLAY PUBLISHING CO.,

VALLEY FALLS, KANSAS.

E. M., 289. (1889.)

TO THE POOR

IN GREAT CITIES AND AGRICULTURAL DISTRICTS,

DWELLERS IN STIFLING COURT OR CROWDED

HOVEL,

IN THE HOPE

THAT IT MAY POINT OUT A PATH FROM POVERTY, AND

MAY MAKE EASIER THE LIFE OF

BRITISH MOTHERS,

TO THEM

I DEDICATE THIS ESSAY.

THE LAW OF POPULATION.

CHAPTER I.

THE LAW OF POPULATION.

The law of population first laid down in this country by the Rev. T. R. Malthus in his great work, entitled "The Principle of Population," has long been known to every student, and accepted by every thinker. It is, however, but very recently that this question has become ventilated among the many, instead of being discussed only by the few. Acknowledged as an axiom by the naturalist and by the political economist, the law of population has never been appreciated by the mass of the people. The free press pioneers of the last generation, Richard Carlile, James Watson, Robert Dale Owen—these men had seen its importance and had endeavored, by cheap publications dealing with it from its practical side, to arouse attention and to instruct those for whom they worked. But the lesson fell on stony ground and passed almost unheeded; it would, perhaps, be fairer to say that the fierce political conflicts of the time threw all other questions into a comparative shade; nor must the strong prejudice against Malthus be forgotten—the prejudice which regarded him as a hard, cold theorist, who wrote in the interest of the richer classes, and would deny to the poor man the comfort of wife and home. The books issued at this period—such as Carlile's "Every Woman's Book," Knowlton's "Fruits of Philosophy," R. D. Owen's "Moral Physiology"—passed unchallenged by authority, but obtained only a limited circulation; here and there they did their work, and the result was seen in the greater comfort and respectability of the families who took advantage of their teachings, but the great mass of the people went on in their ignorance and their ever-increasing poverty, conscious that mouths multiply more rapidly than wages, but dimly supposing that Providence was the responsible agent, and that where "God sends mouths" he ought to " send meat."

One or two recognized advocates for the people did not forget the social side of the work which they had inherited; men like Austin Holyoake and Charles Bradlaugh, carrying on the struggle of Carlile and Watson, were not careless of this vital portion of it, and Mr. Holyoake's " Large and Small Families," and Mr. Bradlaugh's declaration that the *National Reformer* was to be "Malthusian" in its political economy, proved that these two, at least, were sound on this scarcely regarded branch of social science.

Now, all has changed; Malthusianism has become one of the "burning questions" of the day, and a low priced work, stating clearly the outlines of the subject, has become a necessity. Our paternal authorities, like their predecessors, entertain a horror of cheap knowledge, but they will have to assent to the circulation of cheap information on social science, as those who went before them were compelled to tacitly assent to cheap information touching kings and priests.

The law of population, tersely stated, is—"there is a tendency in all animated existence to increase faster than the means of subsistence. Nature produces more life than she can support, and the superabundant life is kept down by the want of food. Malthus put the law thus: "The constant tendency in all animated life to increase beyond the nourishment prepared for it." "It is observed by Dr. Franklin," he writes, " that there is no bound to the prolific nature of plants or animals but what is made by their crowding and interfering with each other's means of subsistence. . . . . . .
Throughout the animal and vegetable kingdoms, Nature has scattered the seeds of life abroad with the most profuse and liberal hand; but has been comparatively sparing in the room and the nourishment necessary to rear them." " Population," Malthus teaches, "when unchecked, goes on doubling itself every twenty-five years;" " in the northern States of America, where the means of subsistence have been more ample, the manners of the people more pure, and the checks to early marriages fewer than in any of the modern States of Europe, the population has been found to double itself, for above a century and a half successively, in less than twenty-five years. In the back settlements, where the sole employment is agriculture, and vicious customs and unwholesome occupations are little known, the population has been found to double itself in fifteen years. Even this extraordinary rate of in-

crease is probably short of the utmost power of population."

The "power of increase" of the human species, according to John Stuart Mill, "is indefinite, and the actual multiplication would be extraordinarily rapid, if the power were exercised to the utmost. It never is exercised to the utmost, and yet, in the most favorable circumstances known to exist, which are those of a fertile region colonized from an industrious and civilized community, population has continued for several generations, independently of fresh immigration, to double itself in not much more than twenty years. . . . It is a very low estimate of the capacity of increase, if we only assume that in a good sanitary condition of the people, each generation may be double the number of the generation which preceded it." James Mill wrote: "That population therefore has such a tendency to increase as would enable it to double itself in a small number of years, is a proposition resting on the strongest evidence, which nothing that deserves the name of evidence has been brought on the other side to oppose."

Mr. McCulloch tells us that "it has been established beyond all question that the population of some of the states of North America, after making due allowance for immigration, has continued to double for a century past in so short a period as twenty, or at most five-and-twenty years." M. Moreau de Jonnès gives us the following table of the time in which the population of each of the under-mentioned countries would double itself:—

Turkey	would take	...	...	555	years.
Switzerland	,,	...	...	227	,,
France	,,	...	...	138	,,
Spain	,,	...	...	106	,,
Holland	,,	...	...	100	,,
Germany	,,	...	...	76	,,
Russia	,,	...	...	43	,,
England	,,	...	...	43	,,
United States	,,	...	...	25	,,

(Without reckoning immigrants.)

We shall take but a narrow view of the law of population if we confine ourselves exclusively to human beings. Man is but the highest in the animal kingdom, not a creature apart from it, and the law of population runs through the animal and the vegetable worlds. To take the commonest illustration: the horse is but a slowly breeding animal, producing but one at a birth, and that at considerable intervals of time; yet how small a proportion of the horses of a country are either stallions or brood mares; the reproductive organs of the colt are destroyed in the enormous majority of those born, and, nevertheless, our production of horses suffices for the vast needs of our commercial and luxurious classes. Darwin, in his "Origin of Species," writes:— "There is no exception to the rule that every organic being naturally increases at so high a rate that, if not destroyed, the earth would soon be covered by the progeny of a single pair. Even slow-breeding man has doubled in twenty-five years, and at this rate, in a few thousand years, there would literally not be standing room for his progeny. Linnæus has calculated that if an annual plant produced only two seeds— and there is no plant so unproductive as this—and their seedlings next year produced two and so on, then in twenty years there would be a million plants. The elephant is reckoned the slowest breeder of all known animals, and I have taken some pains to estimate its probable minimum rate of natural increase; it will be under the mark to assume that it breeds when thirty years old, and goes on breeding till ninety years old, bringing forth three pairs of young in this interval; if this be so, at the end of the fifth century there would be alive 15,000,000 elephants, descended from the first pair. But we have better evidence on this subject than mere theoretical calculations, namely, the numerous recorded cases of the astonishingly rapid increase of various animals in a state of nature, when circumstances have been favorable to them during two or three following seasons. Still more striking is the evidence from our domestic animals of many kinds which have run wild in many parts of the world; if the statements of the rate of increase of slow-breeding cattle and horses in South America, and latterly in Australia, had not been well authenticated, they would have been incredible. So it is with plants; cases could be given of introduced plants which have become common throughout whole islands in a period of less than ten years. Several of the plants, such as the cardoon and a tall thistle, now most numerous over the wide plains of La Plata, clothing square leagues of surface almost to the exclusion of all other plants, have been introduced from Europe; and there are plants which now range in India, as I hear from Dr. Falconer, from Cape Comorin to the Himalayas, which have been imported from America since its discovery. In such cases, and endless instances could be given, no one supposes that the fertility of these animals or plants has been suddenly and temporarily increased in any sensible degree. The obvious explanation is that the conditions of life have been very favorable, and that there has consequently been less destruction of the old and young, and that nearly all the young have been enabled to breed. In such cases the geometrical ratio of increase, the result of which never fails to be surprising, simply explains the extraordinarily rapid increase and wide diffusion of naturalized productions in their new homes. In a state of nature almost every plant produces seed, and amongst animals there are very few which do not annually pair. Hence, we may confidently assert that all plants and animals are tending to increase at a geometrical ratio, that all would most rapidly stock every station in which they could anyhow exist, and that the geometrical tendency to increase must be checked by destruction at some period of life."

Mr. John Stuart Mill also remarks: "The power of multiplication inherent in all organic life may be regarded as *infinite*. There is no species of vegetable or animal, which, if the earth were entirely abandoned to it, and to the things on which it feeds, would not in a small number of years overspread every region of the globe of which the climate was compatible with its existence."

The rapid multiplication of rabbits in Australia has lately given a startling instance of reproductive power; a number of rabbits were taken over and let loose; the district was thinly peopled, so they were not shot down to any great extent; their natural enemies, the hawks, weasels, &c., that prey on their young in England, were not taken over with them; food was abundant, and there was no check to keep them back; the consequence was that whole districts were overrun by them, and the farmers were at their wits' end to save their crops from the swarming rodents. In France, again, owing to the wholesale destruction of small birds, there was a perfect plague of insects, and the inhabitants of many districts have striven to import birds, so as to prevent the insects from practically destroying the vegetation.

While in the vegetable and animal kingdoms the rapidity of the increase is generally far greater than in the human race, we have yet seen how rapidly man has been found to increase where the circumstances surrounding him were favorable to vigorous life. We have never yet, however, seen the full power of reproduction among mankind; the increase of population in America "falls very far short," says the author of the "Elements of Social Science," "of the possible rate of increase, as is seen by the short average of life in America, and by the large amount of the reproductive power which, even in that country, is lost from celibacy and prostitution. . . . The capacity of increase in the human race, as in all other organized beings, is, in fact, boundless and immeasurable."

But while animated existence increases thus rapidly no such swift multiplication can be secured of the means of subsistence. The means of subsistence of vegetable life are strictly limited in quantity; the amount obtainable from the soil may be increased by manure, by careful tillage, by rotation of crops, by improved methods of husbandry, but none the less is this amount limitable, while there is no limit to the power of animal life-production; if the soil and air and light could be indefinitely stretched, vegetable life would still suffice without effort to clothe the increased surface. But since the size of the globe inexorably limits the amount of vegetable produce possible of growth, the limited vegetable produce must, in its turn, limit the amount of animal life which can be sustained. While increased knowledge, skill and care may augment the means of subsistence obtainable from the earth, yet animal life multiplies more rapidly than can its food. As is truly said by the author just quoted: " From a consideration of the law of agricultural industry, and an estimate of the rate at which the means of subsistence could be increased in old countries, even under the most favorable circumstances, it may be inferred with certainty that these means of subsistence could not possibly be increased so fast as to permit population to increase at its natural rate. . . Let us apply the American rate of increase to the population of this country. Is it conceivably possible that the population of England or any old country should double itself every twenty-five years? In Great Britain there are now" (the book was written many years ago) "about twenty-one-millions; is it conceivable that the means of subsistence could be so rapidly increased as to allow these twenty-one millions to swell to forty-two millions in the first twenty-five years; to eighty-four millions in the next; 168 millions in the next, &c.? The supposition is evidently absurd. Even the rate of increase of the last fifty-three years (in which time the population has doubled) cannot possibly be long continued. If it were, it would increase our population in three centuries to about 1300 millions; or, in other words, to more than the total population of the globe, which is estimated at about 1000 millions."

Wherever, then, we look throughout Nature we find proofs of the truth of the law, that "there is a tendency in all animated existence to increase faster than the means of subsistence." This is the law of which Miss Martineau said that it could be no more upset than a law of arithmetic; this is the law which John Stuart Mill regarded "as axiomatic;" this is the law which the Lord Chief Justice designated "an irrefragable truth." Controversialists may quarrel as to its consequences, and may differ as to man's duty in regard to them, but no controversy can arise on the law itself, any more than on the sphericity of the earth.

CHAPTER II.

ITS CONSEQUENCES.

It is abundantly clear, from experience, that population does not, as a general rule, increase at anything like the rate spoken of in the preceding chapter; the earth would, long ere now, have become unable to support her offspring, if they had multiplied at the pace which the naturalist tells us is possible; if, for instance, all rabbits had increased in the same ratio as those taken over to Australia and naturalized there. Some cause must therefore be at work checking the increase and preventing over-rapid multiplication, holding the balance, in fact, roughly even between the means of subsistence and the living creatures who consume them. In the vegetable kingdom the checks to increase are not difficult to find; every plant needs for its development suitable soil, moisture, air, and light; these are its means of subsistence. The amount of these is limited, while the power of multiplication in the vegetable is unlimited. What is the necessary consequence? That of the myriad seeds produced only a few will develop into seed-bearing plants; each seed needs a certain proportion of soil, moisture, air, light; if they fall round the parent stem and sprout into seedlings, they so crowd each other that the weaker perish; every gardener knows that his seedlings need thinning if any are to grow into useful plants, that his plantations must be thinned out, if any tree is to have full development; an overcrowded plantation, an overcrowded garden-bed, gives a crop of dwarfed, stunted, weak, and useless plants. These facts are so commonplace that they pass continually before our eyes, and the simple inference from them is unregarded. There is another check of a severe character on vegetable increase. Birds eat the seeds; animals browse on the plants; man uses many kinds for his own support; the wheat sown in one year, not only produces the seed corn for the ensuing season, but also affords so vast a multiplication as to supply the world with bread; the animal world preys on the vegetable, and so is made a check which destroys the mature, as well as the check of want of room and nourishment which destroys the infant, growth. Out of 357 seedlings of English weeds, carefully watched by Mr. Darwin, 295 were destroyed. On some heaths near Farnham, in the portions enclosed during ten years previously, self-sown firs were observed by him springing up so closely that all could not live, while in the unenclosed portions not one young tree was to be seen. On close examination Mr. Darwin found, in one square yard, thirty-two little trees, no higher than the heather, one with twenty-six rings of growth: the check here was the browsing of cattle over the open parts of the heath. In the animal kingdom the same class of checks is found: the rabbit which in Australia has become an intolerable plague, is kept down to a fair level in England, not because he multiplies less rapidly, but because the check of destruction is brought to bear upon him; food is scarcer in the more cultivated land; guns and traps send him to the market in millions; hawks, weasels, cats, prey upon his young; he produces life rapidly, but the check of death waits upon him and keeps him down. The swift increase of plants and animals under favorable circumstances, dealt with in Chapter I., shows the enormous power of the destructive checks which generally keep in subjection the life-producing force. Once more turning to Mr. Darwin, we read:—

"Of the many individuals of any species which are periodically born, but a small number can survive. . . . A struggle for existence inevitably follows from the high rate at which all organic beings tend to increase. Every being, which during its natural lifetime produces several eggs or seeds, must suffer destruction during some period of its life, and during some season or occasional year, otherwise, on the principle of geometrical increase, its numbers would quickly become so inordinately great that no country could support the product. Hence, as more individuals are produced than can possibly survive, there must in every case be a struggle for existence, either one individual with another of the same species, or with the individuals of distinct species, or with the physical conditions of life. It is the doctrine of Malthus applied with manifold force to the whole animal and vegetable kingdoms; for in this case there can be no artificial increase of food, and no prudential restraint from marriage. Although some species may be now increasing more or less rapidly in numbers, all cannot do so, for the world would not hold them. . . . Our familiarity with the larger domestic animals tends, I think, to mislead us; we see no great destruction falling on them, and we forget that thousands are annually slaughtered for food, and that in a state of nature an equal number would have somehow to be disposed of. . . In looking at nature, it is most necessary to keep the foregoing considerations always in mind—never to forget that every single organic being around us may be said to be striving to the utmost to increase in numbers; that each lives by a struggle at some period of its life; that heavy destruction inevitably falls either on the young or old during each generation or at recurrent intervals. Lighten any check, mitigate the destruction ever so little, and the number of the species will almost instantaneously increase to any amount."

If there be such vast destruction of life throughout the vegetable and animal kingdoms, necessarily consequent on the superabundance of life produced, is man exempt from the same law?

Malthus laid down the three following propositions, propositions of which his book is only an amplification :—

" 1. Population is necessarily limited by the means of subsistence.

" 2. Population invariably increases where the means of subsistence increase, unless prevented by some very powerful and obvious checks.

" 3. These checks, and the checks which repress the superior power of population, and keep its effects on a level with the means of subsistence, are all resolvable into moral restraint, vice, and misery.

" The ultimate check to population appears to be a want of food, arising necessarily from the different ratios according to which population and food increase. But this ultimate check is never the immediate check. except in cases of actual famine. The immediate check may be stated to consist in all those customs and all those diseases, which seem to be generated by a scarcity of the means of subsistence; and all those causes, independent of this scarcity, whether of a moral or physical nature, which tend prematurely to weaken and destroy the human frame." These causes which retard the growth of population by killing human beings, either slowly or rapidly, are all classed together by Malthus under the head of "positive" checks; they are the "natural" checks to population, common alike to vegetables, to animals, to man; they are all checks of suffering, of want, of disease; they are life-destroying, anti-human, brutal, irrational.

These checks are, as might be imagined, more striking, more openly repulsive, more thorough, among savage than among civilized nations. War, infanticide, hardship, famine, disease, murder of the aged, all these are among the positive checks which keep down the increase of population among savage tribes. War carries off the young men, full of vigor, the warriors in their prime of life, the strongest, the most robust, the most fiery—those, in fact, who, from their physical strength and energy would be most likely to add largely to the number of the tribe. Infanticide, most prevalent where means of existence are most restricted, is largely practiced among barbarous nations the custom being due, to a great extent, to the difficulty of providing food for a large family. Hardship carries away many a child in savage life: "Women," says Malthus, "obliged, by their habits of living, to a constant change of places, and compelled to an unremitting drudgery for their husbands, appear to be absolutely incapable of bringing up two or three children nearly of the same age. If another child be born before the one above it can shift for itself, and follow its mother on foot, one of the two must almost necessarily perish from want of care." Famine, so easily caused among a primitive community, sweeps off young and old together; epidemics carry away almost a whole tribe at one swoop; the aged are often slain, or left to perish, when their feebleness no longer permits them to add to the productive force of the community.

All these miseries are the positive and natural checks to population among uncivilized beings; among the more civilized the checks are the same in kind although more decently veiled. But the moment we come among civilized nations a new factor is introduced into the problem which complicates it very considerably. Hitherto we have seen Nature--apart from man—going her own way, producing and destroying without let or hindrance. But when we examine civilized nations we find a new agent at work; Nature's grandest product, the brain of man, now comes into play, and a new set of circumstances arises. Men, women, and children, who would be doomed to death in the savage state, have their lives prolonged by civilization; the sickly, whom the hardships of the savage struggle for existence would kill off, are carefully tended in hospitals, and saved by medical skill; the parents, whose thread of life would be cut short, are cherished on into prolonged old age; the feeble, who would be left to starve, are tenderly shielded from hardship, and life's road is made the smoother for the lame; the average of life is lengthened, and more and more thought is brought to bear on the causes of preventable disease; better drainage, better homes, better food, better clothing, all these, among the more comfortable classes, remove many of the natural checks to population. Among these nations wars become less frequent and less bloody; famines, owing to improved means of inter-communication, become for a time almost impossible; epidemics no longer depopulate whole districts. In England, in A. D. 1258, no less than 15,000 people were starved to death in London alone; in France, in A. D. 1348, one-third of the whole population perished from the same cause; in Rome, from A. D. 250-265, a plague raged, that, for some time, carried off daily 5 000 persons; in England, in A. D. 1506 and 1517, the sweating sickness slew half the inhabitants of the large towns and depopulated Oxford; in London, in A. D. 1603-4, the plague killed 30,578 persons, and in A D. 1664-5 it destroyed 68,596; in Naples, in A. D 1656, 400,000 died and in Egypt, A. D. 1792, above 800,000. These terrible epidemics and famines have ceased to sweep over Europe, but for how long? This decrease of natural checks to population, consequent on advancing civilization, has, unfortunately, a very dark side. Darwin has remarked: "Lighten any check, mitigate the destruction ever so little, and the number of the species will almost instantaneously increase to any amount." A signal instance of the truth of this remark is now being given to us in our Indian empire by the introduction there of Western civilization; Lord Derby says: 'We have established there order and peace; we have done away with local wars; we have lessened the ravages of pestilence; and we do what we can—and, in ordinary seasons, we do it with success—to mitigate the effects of destitution. The result is, naturally and necessarily, a vast increase in population; and if present appearances can be trusted, we shall have in every generation a larger aggregate of human beings relying upon us for help in those periods of distress which must, from time to time, occur in a country wholly agricultural and liable to droughts." So that it appears that our civilization in India, taking away the ordinary natural checks to population, *and introducing no others in their stead*, brings about a famine which has already destroyed more than 500,000 people in one Presidency alone, and has thrown about one and a half million more on charity. From this point of view civilization can scarcely be regarded as an unmixed blessing, and it must not be forgotten that what is happening in India now must, sooner or later, happen in every country where science destroys the balance of nature.

Ireland suffered thirty years ago from exactly the same cause which has now touched India—over-population. Professor Fawcett, in his Essay on Pauperism, writes as follows:—"Ireland should serve to warn us of the terrible misfortunes brought upon a country by an undue increase of population. At the beginning of the eighteenth century, the population of that country was about two millions; maintaining for the next 150 years a smaller rate of increase than is now going on in England, the two millions had grown into eight millions in the year 1847. The country, at this time, became so densely peopled that a considerable portion of the nation could only obtain the barest subsistence; still nothing was done to avert the suffering that was certain to ensue; the people went on marrying with as much recklessness as if they were the first settlers in a new country possessing a boundless area of fertile land. All the influence that could be exerted by religion prompted the continuance of habits of utter improvidence; the priests and other ministers of religion encouraged early marriages. At length there came one of those unpropitious seasons which are certain occasionally to recur; the potato, the staple food of the people, was diseased, and it was soon found that there were more people in the country than could be fed."

Here, again, we see famine as the result of improved civilization. Turning to England, we find that our population is growing rapidly enough to cause anxiety; although there are some severe checks, with which we shall deal presently England has almost doubled her population during the last fifty years. In 1810 the population of England and Wales was about 10,000,000, and in 1860 it was about 20,000,000. "At the present time," writes Professor Fawcett, "it is growing at the rate of 200,000 every year, which is almost equivalent to the population of the county of Northampton. If in fifty years the descendants of one million become two millions, it is obvious that in 100 years the two millions will have become four millions, so that if the population of England were eight millions in 1810 it would be 80 millions in 1960." 40 years hence, if we maintain the rate of increase which we have kept up since the commencement of this century, some 40 millions of people will be crowded into our little island; yet "at the present time it is said that there is a great redundancy of labor. Many who are willing to work cannot find employment; in most of our important branches of industry there has been great over-production; every trade and every profession is over-crowded; for every vacant clerkship there are hundreds of applications. Difficult as it is for men to obtain a livelihood, it is ten times more difficult for women to do so; partly on account of unjust laws, and partly because of the tyranny of society, they are shut out from many employments. All that has just been stated is admitted by common consent—it is the topic of daily conversation, and of daily complaint—and yet with the utmost complacency we observe 200,000 added to our population every year, and we often congratulate ourselves upon this addition to our numbers, as if it were an unerring sign of advancing prosperity. But viewed in relation to the facts just mentioned, what does this addition to our numbers indicate? To this question only one reply can be given—that in ten years' time, where there are a hundred now seeking employment there will then be a hundred and twenty. This will not apply simply to one industry, but will be the case throughout the whole country. It will also further happen that in ten years' time for every hundred that now require food, fuel, and clothing, a similar provision will have to be made for one hundred and twenty. It therefore follows that, low as the general average standard of living now is, it cannot by any means be obtained, unless in ten years' time the supply of all the commodities of ordinary consumption can be increased by 20 per cent., without their becoming more costly." The continually rising price of food is one of the most certain signs that population in England is pressing over hard on the means of subsistence; although our own corn and meat production is enormously supplemented by supplies from abroad, prices are always going up, and the large amount of adulteration practiced in every food-supplying trade is, to a great extent, an effort to equalize the supply and the demand. Much of the food on which our poor live is unwholesome in the extreme ; let anyone walk through the poorer districts of London, or of any large town and see the provisions lying for sale in the shops ; it is not only the meat sold for cooking at home, the doubtful sugar and not doubtful apology for butter, the blue milk, the limp and flabby vegetables—but let the inquirer stop at the cook-shop and inspect the fish, unpleasant both to eye and smell, in itself and in its cooking ; the " faggots" —the eating of which killed a child the other day; the strangely shaped and strangely marked lumps of what should be meat, and, after an hour's walk, the searcher will not wonder at the wan, haggard faces of those who support life on this untempting fare. Even of this fare, however, there is not enough; the low fever so sadly common in poor districts, the " falling away," the hollow cough, the premature old age, all these are the results of insufficiency of food—insufficiency which does not kill at once, but slowly and surely starves away the life. Much of the drunkenness, most common in the poorer districts, has its root in lack of food; the constantly craving stomach is stilled with drink, which it would not desire if it were better filled.

But the pressure on the means of subsistence has other consequences than the living on unwholesome food. One of the earliest signs of too rapidly increasing population is the over-crowding of the poor. Just as the over-crowded seedlings spoil each other's growth, so do the overcrowded poor injure each other morally, mentally, and physically. Whether we study town or country the result of our inquiries is the same—the houses are too small and the families are too large. Take, as illustrating this, the terrible instances given by Mr. George Godwin in his essay on " Over-crowding in London." In Lincoln Court he states that : " In the majority of the houses the rooms are small, and the staircases are narrow and without ventilation. In two of them it was admitted that more than thirty-five persons lived in each; but it would probably be nearer truth to say that each house of eight rooms contains on an average, including children, forty-five persons." " A child was found dead in Brownlow Street, and on inquiry, it was learnt that the mother, a widow, and six children slept in one bed in a small room. The death of the child was attributed to the bedclothes." "In a model lodging house for families, a father, who with his wife and one child occupies one room, has accommodated six of his nine other children the crossway on two camp bedsteads, while three elder girls, one sixteen years old, sleep on a small bedstead near." "In a respectable house not far from the last, occupied by steady artisans and others, I found that nine persons slept in one of the rooms (12 feet by 14 feet), a father, mother and seven children. Eleven shoemakers worked in the attics; and in each of the other five rooms there was a separate family. I could quote scores of such cases of overcrowding in what would seem to be decent houses." "Hundreds of modern houses, built in decent suburban neighborhoods, as if for one family only, are made to contain several. The neat external appearance of many of them gives no suggestion of the dangerously-crowded state of the houses. A description of one of them in Bemerton Street, Caledonian Road, will be more truthful. The basement below the level of the street contains in the front room an old man and his wife; in the back room, two lodgers; in the parlors there are a man and his wife and eight children. On the first floor, a man and his wife and infant; two girls, sixteen and eighteen years of age, and occasionally their mother—all in the front room; and in the small back room, two women, a girl, and two young children. On the second floor, a father, mother, two grown up sons, an infant, and a brood of rabbits. Two women and two boys in the back room make the whole population of the house thirty four. In the next there were thirty-three persons similarly divided." "In one small house, with staircase in the centre, there were in the four small rooms on each side of it, forty persons in the daytime. How many there may be at night I cannot say. The atmosphere on the staircase was sickening." Who can wonder that the death-rate is so high in large cities, and that the difference in the death-rate between the rich and poor sections of the same city is appalling. In Glasgow, for the quarter ending June 30, the death rate in the Blythswood division was 19; that in the Bridgegate and Wynds division 52¹. Many of the deaths in the richer districts might be prevented by better sanitary arrangements and wider sanitary knowledge; the excess in the poorer districts is clearly preventable with our present knowledge, and preventable death is manslaughter. As might be expected, the rate of infant mortality is very high in these overcrowded districts; where 200 children under the age of five years die among the rich, 600 die among the poor; a young child is easily killed, and the bad air and unwholesome food rapidly murder the little ones; again quoting from the Glasgow report, "a large number of the deaths, bearing the relation of $13\frac{1}{2}$ per cent. to the total births, were those of children under one year." In addition to the actual deaths caused by overcrowding, we must add to the mass of misery accruing from it, the non-fatal diseases and the general debility and lack of vigorous life so common in our large centres of industry. "Overcrowding," says Mr. Godwin, "means want of pure air; and want of pure air means debility, continued fever, death, widowhood, orphanage, pauperism, and money loss to the living." Epidemics are most fatal in over-crowded districts, not only because they pass so rapidly from one to another, but also because the people dwelling in those districts have less vitality, less vigor of resistance, than those more fortunately circumstanced. "The great reason," said Dr. Drysdale in the late trial in the Court of Queen's Bench, "that typhus fever is so terrible a disease is that people are crowded. It is impossible to have health with large crowded families." Here then is one of the commonest checks to population in all great cities. Nor must the results to morality be omitted in this imperfect summary of the evils which grow out of over-crowding. What modesty, what decency, what self-respect is possible to these men and women, boys and girls, herded together, seven, ten, fourteen in a room? Only the absence of these virtues could make the life endurable for four-and-twenty hours; no delicacy of feeling can exist there, and we cannot wonder at Dr. Drysdale's sad answer in the recent trial: "They do not know what modesty is."

Can there be any doubt that it is the large families so common among the English poor that are the root of this over-crowding? For not only would the "model-lodging house" spoken of above have been less crowded if the parents, instead of having ten children, had had only two, but with fewer children less money would be needed for food and clothing, and more could be spared for rent. The artisan with six children, forced to live in a stifling pair of rooms in a back street in London in order to be near his work, might, if he had only two, spare money enough to pay his rail to and fro from the suburbs, where the same rent would give him decent accommodation; and not only would he have a better home, but the two children would grow strong in the free air, where the six pine in the London street, and the two would have plenty of food and clothing, where the six lack both. Mr. Godwin recognizes this fact; he says: "Amongst the causes which lead to the evil we are deploring, we must not overlook the gradual increase of children, while in the case of the laboring man, the income mostly remains the same. . . . As the children increase in number the wife is prevented from adding by her earnings to the income, and many years must elapse before the children can be put to work." "Ought to be put to work," would be a truer phrase, for the age at which young children are forced to help in winning their daily bread is one of the disgraces of our civilization.

Overcrowding in country districts is, naturally, not so injurious to health as it is in the towns; the daily work in the open air, the fresh breeze blowing round the cottage, and cleansing, to some extent, the atmosphere within, the fields and lanes where the children can play, all these things may do much to neutralize the harm to health wrought by overcrowding at night. The injury to health, caused by large families among the agricultural poor, arises more from other causes than from overcrowding; the low wage cannot afford a house sufficiently good, and the cheap ill-built cottage, damp, draughty, badly-drained, brings to those who live in it the fever, and the ague, and the rheumatism so sadly common among these laboring classes. But the moral effect of overcrowding is, as the present Bishop of Manchester said—when serving, as the Rev. J. Fraser, in the Royal Commission on the employment of children, young persons, and women in agriculture—"fearful to contemplate." "Modesty," he goes on, "must be an unknown virtue, decency an unimaginable thing, where, in one small chamber, with the beds lying as thickly as they can be packed, father, mother, young men, lads, grown and growing up girls—two and sometimes three generations—are herded promiscuously; where every operation of the toilette and of nature—dressings, undressings, births, deaths—is performed by each within the sight or hearing of all; where children of both sexes, to as high an age as twelve or fourteen, or even more, occupy the same bed; where the whole atmosphere is sensual, and human nature is degraded into something below the level of the swine."

The too early putting of the children to work is one of the consequences of over-large families. In the country the children working in gangs in the fields learn evil speech and evil act at an age when they should be innocent. at school and at play. In town, in the factory and in the workroom, the seeds of disease are sown in the child laborers. "Children in big families," says Dr. Drysdale, "are taken out to work very early, and premature exertion often injures them for life. . . Children are not fit to do very much work so long as they are half developed, and early death is often the consequence." Children should not work for their bread; the frame is not fit for toil, the brain is not ready for the effort of long attention; those who give the life should support and protect it until the tenderness of childhood is passed away, and the young body is firm-knit and strong, prepared to take its share of the battle, and bear the burden and heat of the day.

From the same pressure and struggle for existence, consequent on the difficulty of winning the means of life in an over-crowded land, arise the unhealthy conditions among which many kinds of work are carried on. Mr. Godwin remarks, as to artificial flower-making: "In an upper room in Oxford Street, not ten feet square, I have seen a dozen delicate young women closely shut up, pursuing this occupation. . . . . Many of the workrooms of fashionable milliners are similarly over-c owded, as are those where young girls are engaged in book stitching. Take, as an example, a hou e in Fleet Street, looked at not long ago The passage is narrow; a door in it shuts with a spring; the staircase is confined and without ventilation; the atmosphere is steamy and smells of glue; ascending, it is seen that all the doors shut with springs. In the first room looked into forty young women and girls were sorting and stitching books. . . . . Poor creatures so placed are being slowly slain.' Dr Symes Thompson. writing on the "Influence of Occupation on Health and Life," points out the death bringing circumstances under which too many of our wealth-producers toil; if there were fewer of them their lives would be more valuable than they are; horses and cattle are cared for and protected; the very machinery used is oiled and polished; only the human machines are worked under life-ruining conditions, and are left to struggle on as best they may. Dr. Thompson gives cases of printers – which every one connected with journalism can supplement by his own experience – where unwholesome atmosphere and preposterously long hours destroy the constitution. He tells us how the shoddy-grinders, the cocoa-matting weavers, the chaff cutters, the workers in flax, woolen, and cotton factories, suffer from a 'peculiar kind of bronchitis, arising from the irritation of the dust" and other matters inhaled, and the cough "is followed by expectoration, and, if the occupation is continued, emphysema, or, in those predisposed to phthisis, tubercle is developed." At Sheffield the "inhalation of metal filings" is "destructive" to the knife and fork grinders, and although this might be prevented by the use of respirators the men s lives are not sufficiently valuable to be thus saved. If grit got into the works of a machine and ruined them the works would be covered over, but it may pass into men's lungs and kill them and no one troubles. Brass finishers and stone-masons labor under the same disadvantages; lead poisoning is common among plumbers, painters, &c.; "women employed in lead works rarely bear healthy children; in a large number of cases miscarriage occurs at the fifth or seventh month, and if the children are born alive they rarely survive long Lead exerts a similar influence on the reproductive powers in the male sex; men with lead affections seldom produce healthy children." Many of these diseases might be prevented, if the excessive number of workers did not make the prevention a matter of indifference to those concerned. Dr. Thompson says: "Let over-crowding and over-heating be avoided. There should be an abundant supply of pure air. The hours of work should be moderate, with fair intervals for meals. If there is much dust or other foreign matter in the air a suitable respirator should be used, or the offensive particles should be carried off by a current of air produced by a chimney or revolving wheel. Again, mechanical appliances may often take the place of hand-labor, and much may often be accomplished by the application of practical science and chemical knowledge." Thus we see indifference to life resulting from the overcrowding of the labor market, and in the unhealthy conditions among which many kinds of work are carried on we find a widely-spread check to population.

Baby farming has only too justly been called the "hideous social phenomenon of the nineteenth century." It is the direct result of the pressure of over-large families, and is simply a veiled form of infanticide. Mr. Benson Baker, one of the medical officers of Marylebone, has written a sad notice of baby-farming. He speaks of a notorious case: "One of the stock from that model baby-farm is now under my care. This child, three years old, was employed by the proprietoress as a gaffer or ganger over the younger babies. His duties were to sit up in the middle of the bed with eight other babies round him, and the moment any one of them awoke to put the bottle to their mouth. He was also to keep them quiet, and generally to superintend them." A vast number of children are slowly murdered annually in this way, and the death-rate is also very high in every place where many infants are kept together, whether it be in workhouse, hospital, or crèche.

Another consequence of large families which must not be overlooked is the physical injury caused to the mothers. Among the poor, cases of *prolapsus uteri*, or falling of the womb, are only too common ; *prolapsus uteri* results frequently from "getting about" too rapidly after child birth, it being impossible for the mother of the increasing family to lie by for that period of rest which nature absolutely enjoins. "Women," says Dr. Drysdale, " ought never to get up from confinement for some weeks after the child is born, but these poor women are so utterly unable to do without work that they are compelled to get up in a day or two. The womb being full of blood, falls down and produces infirmity for life." The doctor also says of this disease : " It is extremely common. Indeed, when I was obstetrical assistant at Edinburgh, it was one of the commonest diseases among women—the principal one, in fact." "Prolapsus, or falling of the womb," says Dr. Graily Hewett, "is an affection to which women are in one form or other exceedingly liable, and it is one which is not unfrequently productive of very much inconvenience and distress." The reason of the disease is not far to see. The womb, in its unimpregnated state, is " from two and a half to three inches long, and an inch and a half wide, more or less, at its largest part, and about an inch thick " (Dr. Marion Sims). During the nine months of pregnancy this organ is stretched more and more, until at the end of nine months it is capable of containing the fully developed infant. During these nine months the muscular substance of the womb "increases in thickness, while the whole organ enlarges in order to accommodate the growing fœtus and its appendages " (Dr. Dalton). At birth the muscular fibres begin to contract, and the womb ought to return to almost its original size. But in order that it may so return the horizontal position is absolutely necessary for some days, and much rest for some weeks, until the muscles connected with the womb have regained something of their natural elasticity. If the mother be forced to leave her bed too early, if she be compelled to exert herself in housekeeping cares, to stand over the washtub, to bend over the fire--what happens? The womb so long distended, has no chance of healthy contraction; the muscles which support it in its proper position have not recovered from the long strain; the womb itself is heavy with the blood flowing from the vessels yet unclosed, and it naturally falls and " produces infirmity for life." Too frequent pregnancy is another cause of *prolapsus uteri*, and of many other diseases of the womb. " We frequently find that the uterus becomes diseased from the fact that the pregnancies rapidly succeed each other, the uterus not having recovered its natural size when it becomes again occupied by an ovum " (Dr. Graily Hewett). The womb is too constantly put on the stretch, and is not allowed sufficient rest to recover its original vigor and elasticity. It takes about two months for the womb to thoroughly reconstruct itself after the delivery of a child; a new mucous membrane develops, and a degeneration and reconstruction of the muscles takes place, technically known as "the involution of the uterus." During pregnancy, the uterine muscles " increase very considerably in size. Their texture becomes much more distinctly granular, and their outlines more strongly marked. . . . . . The entire walls of the uterus, at the time of delivery, are composed of such muscular fibres, arranged in circular, oblique, and longitudinal bundles. About the end of the first week after delivery, these fibres begin to undergo a fatty degeneration. . . . The muscular fibres which have become altered by the fatty deposit, are afterwards gradually absorbed and disappear; their place being subsequently taken by other fibres of new formation, which already begin to make their appearance before the old ones have been completely destroyed. As this process goes on, it results finally in a complete renovation of the muscular substances of the uterus. The organ becomes again reduced in size, compact in tissue, and of a pale ruddy hue, as in the ordinary unimpregnated condition. This entire renewal or reconstruction of the uterus is completed, according to Heschl, about the end of the second month after delivery" (Dr. Dalton). No words can add strength to this statement, proving the absolute right of women to complete repose from sexual disturbance during this slow recovery of the normal condition of the womb. Many a woman in fairly comfortable circumstances suffers from lack of knowledge of physical laws, and from the reckless English disregard of all conjugal prudence; short of absolute displacement of the womb, and of grave uterine diseases, various disorders result from weakness of the over taxed generative organs. Leucorrhœa is one of the commonest of these, producing general debility, pain in the back, indigestion, &c It is not right, it is not moral, that mothers of families should thus ruin their health, causing suffering to themselves and misery to those around them; it is only a perverted moral sense which leads men and women to shut their eyes to these sad consequences of over-large families, and causes them thus to disregard the plainest laws of health Sexual intemperance, the over-procreation of children, is as immoral as intemperance in drink.

Among the melancholy consequences of over-population we must not omit the foolish and sometimes criminal attempts made by ignorant people to limit the family; the foolish attempt is the prevalent habit of over-lactation, arising from the mistaken idea that conception is impossible during the nursing of a child; the criminal attempt is the procuring of abortion by means of drugs or by the use of instruments These will be more fully dealt with in Chapter III., and are only alluded to here as among the consequences of the pressure of over-population. Too often, indeed, do these come under the head of the positive, the life destroying checks.

To turn to a different and more immediately life-destroying class of checks, that of war cannot, of course, be left out of this melancholy picture. The Franco-German war, in 1870 the Turco-Russian war now going on, have both been sensible checks to the populations of their respective countries. The great famine now raging in India is a positive check on a still more frightful scale, and we have seen that this terrible famine results entirely from over-population; the evidence of Lord Derby may be taken as conclusive upon this point: but is it possible to accept Lord Derby's facts, and yet make no kind of effort to solve the question which, he says, "does not seem to me to be a light one?" It is all very well to say that: "If present appearances can be trusted, we shall have in every generation a larger aggregate of human beings relying upon us for help in those periods of distress which must from time to time occur in a country wholly agricultural and liable to droughts."

But what a confession of helplessness! Is it possible to sit down with folded hands and calmly contemplate the recurrence at regular intervals of such a famine as is now slaying its tens of thousands? Yet the law of population is "an irrefragable truth," and these people are starved to death, according to natural law; early marriages, large families, these are the premises; famine and disease, these are the conclusions. The same consequences will, sooner or later—sooner in an agricultural country, dependent on its crops, later in a manufacturing country commanding large foreign supplies, but always inexorably—produce the same fearful results.

One more melancholy positive check must be added, the last to which we shall here refer. It is the absolute child-murder by desertion or by more violent means: Dr. Lankester said that "there were in London alone 16,000 women who had murdered their offspring." Dr. Attwood lately stated of Macclesfield that the doctors in that town often had moral, though not legal, proof that children were "put away," and that Macclesfield was "no worse than any other manufacturing town."

Such are some of the consequences of the law of population; the power of production is held in check by the continual destruction, the number of births is balanced by the number of deaths. Population struggles to increase, but the want of the means of existence beats it back, and men, women, and children perish in the terrible struggle. The more civilization advances the more hopeless becomes the outlook. The checks imposed by "nature and providence," in which Sir Hardinge Giffard trusts for the prevention of over-population, are being removed, one by one, by science and by civilization. War will be replaced by arbitration, and those who would have fallen victims to it will become fathers of families; sanitary knowledge will bring sanitary improvement, and typhus fever and small-pox will disappear as the plague and black death have done; children will not die in their infancy, and the average length of human life will increase. The life-destroying checks of "nature and providence" will be met with the life-preserving attempts of science and of reason, and population will increase more and more rapidly. What will be the result? Simply this: India to-day is a microcosm of the world of the future, and the statesman of that time will re-echo the words of the present Foreign Secretary with a wider application. Ought we then to encourage positive checks so as to avert this final catastrophe? Ought we to stir up war? Ought we to prevent sanitary improvements? ought we to leave the sickly to die? Ought we to permit infants to perish unaided? Ought we to refuse help to the starving? These checks may be "natural," but they are not human; they may be "providential," but they are not rational. Has science no help for us in our extremity? has reason no solution to this problem? has thought no message of salvation to the poor?

CHAPTER III.

ITS BEARING UPON HUMAN CONDUCT AND MORALS.

To the question that closes the last chapter there *is* an answer; all thinkers have seen that since population increases more rapidly than the means of subsistence, the human brain should be called in to devise a restriction of the population, and so relieve man from the pressure of the struggle for existence. The lower animals are helpless and must needs suffer, and strive, and die, but man, whose brain raises him above the rest of antimated existence, man rational, thoughtful, civilized, he is not condemned to share in the brute struggle, and to permit lower nature to destroy his happiness and his ever-growing rapidity of progress. In dealing with the law of population, as with every other natural law which presses on him unpleasantly, civilized man seeks so to alter the conditions which surround him as to produce a happier result. Thinkers have, therefore, studied the law and its consequences, and have suggested various views of its bearing on human conduct and morals. It was acknowledged that the only way of escape from pauperism and from the misery occasioned by positive checks, was in the limitation of the population within the available means of subsistence, and the problem to be solved was—How shall this be done? Malthus proposed that prevention, or birth-restricting, should be substituted for positive, or life destroying, checks, and that " moral restraint" should supersede "misery and vice." He lays it down as a principle of duty, that no one "is to bring beings into the world for whom he cannot find the means of support." This obligation, he says, is a "duty intelligible to the humblest capacity." But the duty being admitted on all sides, the crucial point is—How is this duty to be fulfilled? Malthus answers:—By delay of marriage. We are bound " not to marry till we have a fair prospect of being able to support our children;" in a right state of society "no man, whose earnings were only sufficient to maintain two children, would put himself in a situation in which he might have to maintain four or five;" a man should "defer marrying, till, by industry and economy, he is in a capacity to support the children that he may reasonably expect from his marriage." Thus marriage—if ever possible to the poor—would be delayed until the middle of life, and the birth-rate would be decreased by a general abstention from marriage until a comparatively late age.

This preventive check would doubtless be an effectual one, but it is open to grave and fatal objections, and would only replace one set of evils by another. If late marriage were generally practised the most melancholy results would follow. The more marriage is delayed, the more prostitution spreads. It is necessary to gravely remind all advocates of late marriage that men do not and will not live single, and all women, and all men who honor women, should protest against a teaching which would inevitably make permanent that terrible social evil which is the curse of civilization, and which condemns numbers of unhappy creatures to a disgraceful and revolting calling. Prostitution is an evil which we should strive to eradicate, not to perpetuate, and late marriage, generally adopted, would most certainly perpetuate it. The state of the streets of our large towns at nightfall is the result of deferred marriage, and marriage is deferred owing to the ever-increasing difficulty of maintaining a large family in anything like comfort.

Mr. Montagu Cookson, writing in the *Fortnightly Review*, says: "If, indeed, we could all become perfect beings, the rule of life deduced by Malthus from the unalterable law of population would be both practicable and safe; as it is, it has a direct tendency to promote the cardinal vice of cities —that of unchastity. The number of women in England who ply the loathsome trade of prostitution is already large enough to people a county, and, as our great thoroughfares show at nightfall, is certainly not diminishing. Their chief supporters justify themselves by the very plea which Malthus uses to enforce the duty of continence, namely, that they are not well enough off to maintain a wife and family. If they could be sure that they could limit the number of their children, so as to make it commensurate with their income, not only would the plea be generally groundless, but I believe it would not be urged, and the so-called social evil would be stormed in i s strongest fortress."

The evi's resulting from late marriage to those who remain really celibate, must not be overlooked in weighing this recommendation of it as a cure for the evils of overpopulation. Celibacy is not natural to men or to women; all bodily needs require their legitimate satisfaction, and celibacy is a disregard of natural law. The asceticism which depises the body is a contempt of nature, and a revolt against her; the morality which upholds virginity as the type of womanly perfection is unnatural; to be in harmony with nature, men and women should be husbands and wives, fathers and mothers, and until nature evolves a neuter sex celibacy will ever be a mark of imperfection. Very clearly has nature marked celibacy with disapproval; the average life of the unmarried is shorter than the average life of the married; the unmarried have a less vigorous physique, are more withered, more rapidly aged, more peevish, more fanciful; "the disordered emotions of persons of both sexes who pass lives of voluntary or enforced celibacy," says Dr. Drysdale in his essay on Prostitution, "is a fact of every-day observation. Their bad temper, fretfulness, and excitability are proverbial." We quote from the same tractate the following opinions: "M. Villamay, in his 'Dictionnarie des Sciences Médicales,' says ' It is assuredly true that absolute and involuntary abstinence, is the most common cause of hysteria.' Again, at a meeting of the Medico-Chirurgical Society, reported in the *Lancet* of February 14, 1859, Mr. Holmes Coote is reported to have said, ' No doubt incontinence was a great sin; but the evils connected with continence were productive of far greater misery to society. Any person could bear witness to this, who had had experience in the wards of lunatic asylums. Again, Sir. Benjamin Brodie, at the Birmingham Social Science Meeting, is reported to have said, in a discussion on prostitution, that ' the evils of celibacy were so great, that he would not mention them; but that they quite equalled those of prostitution!'" M Block informs us that in France out of 100 male lunatics, 65.72 are celibate, 5.61 are widowers, and only 28 67 are married; of 100 female lunatics, 58.16 are celibate, 12.48 are widows, and 29.36 are married. M. Bertillon, dealing with France, Holland, and Belgium, states that men who live celibate lives after twenty have, on an average, six years less of life than those who marry. The same fact holds good as regards married and unmarried women. A long train of formidable diseases results from celibacy—such as spermatorrhœa in the male, chlorosis and hysteria in the female—and no one who desires society to be happy and healthy should recommend late marriage as a cure for the social evils around us. Early marriage is best, both physically and morally; it guards purity, softens the affections, trains the heart, and preserves physical health; it teaches thought for others, gentleness and self control; it makes men gentler and women braver from the contact of differing natures. The children that spring from such marriages—where not following each other too rapidly—are more vigorous and healthy than those born of middle-aged parents, and in the ordinary course of nature the parents of such children live long enough to see them make their start in life, to aid, strengthen, and counsel them at the beginning of their career.

Fortunately, late marriage will never be generally practised in any community; the majority of men and women will never consent to remain single during the brightness of youth, when passion is strongest and feelings most powerful, and to marry only when life is half over and its bloom and its beauty have faded into middle-age. But it is important that late marriage should not even be regarded as desirable, for if it became an accepted doctrine among the thoughtful that late marriage was the only escape from over population, a serious difficulty would arise; the best of the people, the most careful, the most provident, the most intelligent, would remain celibate and barren, while the careless, thoughtless, thriftless ones would marry and produce large families; the evil is found to prevail to some extent even now: the more thoughtful, seeing the misery resulting from large families on low wage, often abstain from marriage, and have to pay heavy poor rates for the support of the thoughtless and their families. The preventive check proposed by Malthus must therefore be rejected, and a wiser solution of the problem must be sought.

Later thinkers, recognising at once the evils of over-population and the evils of late marriage, have striven to find a path which shall avoid both Scylla and Charybdis, and have advocated early marriages and small families. John Stuart Mill has been one of the most earnest of these true friends of the people; in his "Political Economy" he writes: "In a very backward state of society, like that of Europe in the Middle Ages, and many parts of Asia at present, population is kept down by actual starvation. . . In a more improved state, few, even among the poorest of the people, are limited to actual necessaries, and to a bare sufficiency of those; and the increase is kept within bounds, not by excess of deaths but by limitation of births. The limitation is brought about in various ways. In some countries, it is the result of prudent or conscientious self-restraint. There is a condition to which the labouring people are habituated; they perceive that by having too numerous families, they must sink below that condition, or fail to transmit it to their children; and this they do not choose to submit to. The countries in which, so far as is known, a great degree of voluntary prudence has been longest practised on this subject, are Norway and parts of Switzerland. . . In both these countries the increase of population is very slow; and what checks it, is not multitude of deaths, but fewness of births. Both the births and the deaths are remarkably few in proportion to the population; the average duration of life is the longest in Europe; the population contains fewer children, and a greater proportional number of persons in the vigor of life than is known to be the case in any other part of the world. The paucity of births tends directly to prolong life, by keeping the people in comfortable circumstances." Clearly and pointedly Mill teaches "conjugal prudence;" he quotes with approval the words of Sismondi, who was "among the most benevolent of his time and the happiness of whose married life has been celebrated:" "When dangerous prejudices have not become accredited, when a morality contrary to our true duties towards others, and especially towards those to whom we have given life, is not inculcated in the name of the most sacred authority, no prudent man contracts matrimony before he is in a condition which gives him an assured means of living, and no married man has a greater number of children than he can properly bring up." Many other eminent men and women have spoken in the same sense; Professor Leone Levi advocates "prudence as regards the increase of our families." Mrs. Fawcett writes: "Those who deal with this question of pauperism should remember that it is not to be remedied by cheap food, by reductions of taxation, or by economical administration in the departments, or by new forms of government. Nothing will permanently affect pauperism while the present reckless increase of population continues. And nothing will be so likely to check this increase as the imposition by the State on parents of the whole responsibility of maintaining their offspring." Mr. Montagu Cookson says that some may think "prudential restraint after marriage wilder than anything Malthus ever dreamt," but urges that "the numbers of children born after marriage should be limited," and that "such limitation is as much the duty of married persons as the observance of chastity is the duty of those that are unmarried."

It remains, then, to ask how is this duty to be performed? It is clearly useless to preach the limitation of the family, and to conceal the means whereby such limitation may be effected. If the limitation be a duty, it cannot be wrong to afford such information as shall enable people to discharge it.

There are various prudential checks which have been suggested, but further investigation of this intricate subject is sorely needed, and it is much to be wished that more medical men would devote themselves to the study of this important branch of physiology.

The check we will take first in order is that to which Mr. Montagu Cookson alludes in his essay: he says that the family may be limited by "obedience to natural laws which all may discover and verify if they will." The "natural laws" to which Mr. Cookson refers would be, we imagine, the results of observation on the comparative fertility with women of some periods over others. It is well known that the menstrual discharge, or the Catamenia, recurs in normal cases at monthly intervals, during the whole of the fertile period of female life; a woman does not bear children before menstruation has commenced, nor after it has ceased. There are cases on record where women have borne children but have never menstruated, but these are rare exceptions to the general rule; menstruation is the sign of capability of conception, as its cessation is the sign of future disability to conceive. Recent investigators have collected many cases in which "the menstrual period was evidently connected with the maturation and discharge of ova" (Carpenter). "The essential part of the female generative system," says Dr. Carpenter, "is that in which the ova [eggs] are prepared. . . . In the higher animals, as in the human female, the substance of the ovarium is firm and compact, and consists of a nucleated, tough, fibrous connective tissue, with much interspersed fusiform muscular tissue, forming what is known as the *stroma*. . . . As development proceeds the cells . . . multiply, and single cells or groups of cells, round, ovoid, or tubular, come to be enclosed in the tissue of the ovary by delicate vascular processes which shoot forth from the stroma. These cells constitute the primordial ova." These ova gradually mature, and are then discharged from the ovary and pass into the uterus, and on the fertilization of one of them conception depends. Dr. Kirke writes: ' It has long been known that in the so-called oviparous animals, the separation of ova from the ovary may take place independently of impregnation by the male, or even of sexual union. And it is now established that a like maturation and discharge of ova, independently of coition, occurs in mammalia, the periods at which the matured ova are separated from the ovaries and received into the Fallopian tubes being indicated in the lower mammalia by the phenomena of *heat* or *rut;* in the human female by the phenomena of *menstruation.* . . . It may, therefore, be concluded that the two states, heat and menstruation are analogous, and that the essential accompaniment of both is the maturation and extrusion of ova." Seeing, then, that the ova are discharged at the menstrual periods, and that conception depends on the fertilization of the ova by the male, it is obvious that conception will most readily take place immediately before or after menstruation. "It is quite certain that there is a greater aptitude for conception immediately before and after that epoch than there is at any intermediate period" (Carpenter). A woman "is more apt to conceive soon after menstruation than at any other time" (Chavasse). So much is this fact recognized by the medical profession, that in cases of sterility a husband is often recommended only to visit his wife immediately after the cessation of the Catamenia. Since women conceive more easily at this period, the avoidance of sexual intercourse during the few days before and after menstruation has been recommended as a preventive check. Dr. Tyler Smith writes: " In the middle of the interval between the periods, there is little chance of impregnation taking place. The same kind of knowledge is of use, by way of caution, to women who menstruate during lactation, in whom there is a great aptitude to conceive; pregnancy, under such circumstances, would be injurious to the health of the fœtus, the child at the breast, and the mother herself, and therefore should be avoided, if possible." The most serious objection to reliance on this check is that it is not certain. M. Raciborski says that only 6 or 7 per cent. of conceptions take place during this interval, but the 6 or 7 exceptions to the general rule prevent recommendation of the check as thoroughly reliable; we can scarcely say more than that women are far less likely to conceive midway between the menstrual periods than either immediately before or after them.

The preventive check which is so generally practised in France that Dr. Drysdale—with a rarely wide French experience—stated that among the peasantry it was "used universally," and was "practised by almost every male in Paris, and all over the country," is one which depends entirely on the self-control of the man. It consists simply in the withdrawal of the husband previous to the emission of the semen, and is, of course, absolutely certain as a preventive. A few among the French doctors contend that the practice is injurious, more especially to the wife; but they have failed, so far as we can judge, in making out their case, for they advance no proofs in support of their theory, while the universal practice of the French speaks strongly on the other side.

The preventive check advocated by Dr. Knowlton is, on the other hand, entirely in the hands of the wife. It consists in the use of the ordinary syringe immediately after intercourse, a solution of sulphate of zinc or of alum being used instead of water. There is but little doubt that this check is an effective one, a most melancholy proof of its effectiveness being given by Dr. J. C. Barr, who, giving evidence before the Commission on the working of the Contagious Diseases Act, stated:—"Every woman who leaves the hospital is instructed in the best mode of preventing disease. These are cleanliness, injections of alum and sulphate of zinc."

Professor Sheldon Amos, dealing with the same painful subject, refers to this evidence, and quotes Dr. Barr as saying again, "my custom is to instruct them to keep themselves clean, to use injections and lotions." These women are not meant to bear children, they are to be kept "fit for use" by Her Majesty's soldiers.

Apart altogether from this sad, but governmentally authorized use of this check, there are many obvious disadvantages connected with it as a matter of taste and feeling. The same remark applies to the employment of the *baudruche*, a covering used by men of loose character as a guard against syphilitic diseases, and occasionally recommended as a preventive check.

The check which appears to us to be preferable, as at once certain, and in no sense grating on any feeling of affection or of delicacy, is that recommended by Carlile many years ago in his "Every Woman's Book." In order that impregnation should take place, "the absolute contact of the spermatozoa with the ovum is requisite" (Carpenter). The ovum passes from the ovary down the Fallopian tube into the uterus; the spermatozoa, floating in the spermatic fluid, pass upwards through the uterus, and fecundate the ovum either in the uterus, in the tube, or in the ovary itself. To prevent impregnation it is then only necessary to prevent the contact. The neck of the uterus, where it enters the vagina, ends with the *Os uteri*, an orifice varying in shape in different individuals. Through this orifice the male semen must pass in order to fertilize the ovum. To prevent impregnation, pass to the end of the vagina a piece of fine sponge, which should be dipped in water before being used, and which need not be removed until the morning. Dr. Marion Sims, who in cases of retroversion of the uterus constantly used mechanical support to maintain the uterus in its normal position, and so make pregnancy possible, gives much useful information on the various kinds of pessaries. He sometimes used a "small wad of cotton, not more than an inch in diameter," which was "secured with a string for its removal;" this was worn during the day and removed at night. He says that the woman using a pessary should be able "to remove and replace it with the same facility that she would put on and pull off an old slipper." There is, in fact, no kind of difficulty in the use of this check, and it has the great advantage of unobtrusiveness.

There is a preventive check attempted by many poor women which is most detrimental to health, and should therefore never be employed, namely, the too long persistence in nursing one baby, in the hope of thereby preventing the conception of another. *Nursing does not prevent conception.* A child should not be nursed, according to Dr. Chavasse, for longer than nine months; and he quotes Dr. Farr, as follows:—" It is generally recognized that the healthiest children are those weaned at nine months complete. Prolonged nursing hurts both child and mother: in the child, causing a tendency to brain disease, probably through disordered digestion and nutrition; in the mother, causing a strong tendency to deafness and blindness." Dr. Chavasse adds: "If he be suckled after he be twelve months old, he is generally pale, flabby, unhealthy, and rickety; and the mother is usually nervous, emaciated, and hysterical. . . . A child nursed beyond twelve months is very apt, if he should live, to be knock-kneed, and bow-legged, and weak-ankled, to be narrow-chested, and chicken-breasted." If pregnancy occur, and the mother be nursing, the consequences affect alike the mother, the babe, and the unborn child. To nurse under these circumstances, says Dr. Chavasse, "is highly improper, as it not only injures her own health, and may bring on a miscarriage, but it is also prejudicial to her babe, and may produce a delicacy of constitution from which he might never recover."

Another class of checks is distinctly criminal, *i.e.*, the procuring of abortion. Various drugs are taken by women with this intent, and too often their use results in death, or in dangerous sickness. Dr. Fleetwood Churchill gives various methods of inducing labor prematurely, and argues, justly, that where the delivery of a living child at the full time is impossible, it is better to bring on labor than be compelled to perform later either craniotomy or the Cæsarian section. But he goes further: "There are cases where the distortion [of the pelvis] is so great as to render the passage of a seven months' child impossible, and, others still worse, where no reduction of a viable child's bulk will enable it to pass. I do not see why abortion should not be induced at an early period in such cases." And Dr. Churchill quotes Mr. Ingleby as saying: "Premature labor may with great propriety be proposed on pregnancy recurring, assuming the delivery of a living child at term to have already proved impracticable." If there is a chance for the child's life, this is sound advice, but if the delivery of a living child has been proved to be impossible, surely the prevention of conception is far better than the procuring of abortion. The destruction of the fœtus is destruction of life, and it is immoral, where a woman cannot bear a living child, that she should conceive at all.

If this system of preventive checks were generally adopted, how happy would be the result both to the home and to the State! The root of poverty would be dug up, and pauperism would decline and at last vanish. Where now overcrowded hovels stand, would then be comfortable houses; where now the large family starves in rags, the small family would then live on sufficient food, clad in decent raiment; education would replace ignorance, and self-reliance would supersede charity. Where the workhouse now frowns, the busy school would then smile, and care and forethought for the then valuable lives would diminish the dangers of factory and of work-room. Prostitution would cease to flaunt in our streets, and the sacred home would be early built and joyously dwelt in; wedded love would enter the lists against vice, and, no longer the herald of want, would chase her counterfeit from our land. No longer would transmitted diseases poison our youth, nor premature death destroy our citizens. A full possibility of life would open before each infant born into our nation, and there would be room, and love, and cherishing, enough for each new-comer. It remains for England to have all this if she will; but the first upward step towards that happier life will only be taken when parents resolutely determine to limit their family to their means, and stamp with moral disapprobation every married couple who selfishly overcrowd their home, to the injury of the community of which they are a part.

CHAPTER IV.

OBJECTIONS CONSIDERED.

MANY people, perfectly good-hearted, but somewhat narrow-minded, object strongly to the idea of conjugal prudence, and regard scientific checks to population as "a violation of nature's laws, and a frustration of nature's ends." Such people, a hundred years ago, would have applauded the priest who objected to lightning conductors as being an interference with the bolts of Deity; they exist in every age, the rejoicers over past successes, and the timid disapprovers of new discoveries. Let us analyze the argument. "A violation of nature's laws;" this objection is couched in somewhat unscientific phrase; nature's "laws" are but the observed sequences of events; man cannot violate them; he may disregard them, and suffer in consequence; he may observe them, and regulate his conduct so as to be in harmony with them. Man's prerogative is that by the use of his reason he is able to study nature outside himself, and by observation may so control nature, as to make her add to his happiness instead of bringing him misery. To limit the family is no more a violation of nature's laws, than to preserve the sick by medical skill; the restriction of the birth-rate does not violate nature's laws more than does the restriction of the death-rate. Science strives to diminish the positive checks; science should also discover the best preventive checks. "The frustration of nature's ends." Why should we worship nature's ends? Nature flings lightning at our houses; we frustrate her ends by the lightning conductor. Nature divides us by seas and by rivers; we frustrate her ends by sailing over the seas, and by bridging the rivers. Nature sends typhus fever and ague to slay us; we frustrate her ends by purifying the air, and by draining the marshes. Oh! it is answered, you only do this by using other natural powers. Yes, we answer, and we only teach conjugal prudence by balancing one natural force against another. Such study of nature, and such balancing of natural forces, is civilization.

It is next objected that preventive checks are "unnatural" and "immoral." "Unnatural" they are not; for the human brain is nature's highest product, and all improvements on irrational nature are most purely natural; preventive checks are no more unnatural than every other custom of civilization. Raw meat, nakedness, living in caves, these are the *irrational* natural habits; cooked food, clothes, houses, these are the *rational* natural customs. Production of offspring recklessly, carelessly, lustfully, this is irrational nature, and every brute can here outdo us; production of offspring with forethought, earnestness, providence, this is rational nature, where man stands alone. But "immoral." What is morality? It is the greatest good of the greatest number. It is immoral to give life where you cannot support it. It is immoral to bring children into the world when you cannot clothe, feed, and educate them. It is immoral to crowd new life into already over-crowded houses, and to give birth to children wholesale who never have a chance of healthy life. Conjugal prudence is most highly moral, and "those who endeavor to vilify and degrade these means in the eyes of the public, and who speak of them as 'immoral' and 'disgusting,' are little aware of the moral responsibility they incur thereby. As already shown, to reject preventive intercourse is in reality to choose the other three true population checks—poverty, prostitution, and celibacy. So far from meriting reprobation, the endeavour to spread the knowledge of the preventive methods, of the great law of nature which renders them necessary, is in my opinion the very greatest service which can at present be done to mankind " (" Elements of Social Science ").

But the knowledge of these scientific checks would, it is argued, make vice bolder, and would increase unchastity among women by making it safe. Suppose that this were so, it might save some broken hearts and some deserted children; men ruin women and go scatheless, and then bitterly object that their victims escape something of public shame. And if so, are all to suffer, so that one or two, already corrupt in heart, may be preserved from becoming corrupt in act? Are mothers to die slowly that impure women may be held back, and wives to be sacrificed, that the unchaste may be curbed? As well say that no knives must be used because throats may be cut with them; no matches sold because incendiarism may result from them; no pistols allowed because murders may be committed by them. Blank ignorance has some advantages in the way of safety, and if all men's eyes were put out, none would ever be tempted to seduce a woman for her beauty. Let us bring for our women the veil to cover, and the eunuch to guard, and so be at least consistent in our folly and our distrust! But this knowledge would *not* increase unchastity; the women who cou'd thus use it would be solely those who only lack opportunity, not will, to go astray: the means suggested all imply deliberation and forethought; are these generally the handmaids of unchastity? English women are not yet sunk so low that they preserve their loyalty to one, only from fear of the possible consequences of disloyalty; their purity, their pride, their honour, their womanhood, these are the guardians of their virtue, and never from English women's heart will fade the maiden and matronly dignity, which makes them shield their love from all taint of impurity, and bid them only surrender themselves, where the surrender of heart and of pledged faith have led the way. Shame on those who slander England's wives and maidens wi.h the foul thoughts that can only spring from the mind and the lips of the profligate.

Another class of objectors appears: those who argue that there is no need to limit the population, at any rate for a long while to come. Some of these say that there is food enough in the world for all, and point out that the valley of the Mississippi would grow corn enough to feed the present population of the globe. They forget that the *available* means of subsistence are those with which we have to deal. Corn in Nebraska and starving mouths in Lancashire are not much use to each other; when the cost of carriage exceeds the money power of the would-be buyer, the corn-fields might be in the moon for all the good they are to him; if means can be discovered of bringing corn and mouths together, well and good, but until they are discovered, undue production of mouths here is unwise, because their owners will starve while the corn is still on the other side of the sea.

But if the corn can't be brought to the mouths may not the mouths go to the corn? Why not emigrate? Because emigration is impracticable to the extent needed for the relief of the labour market. Emigration caused by starvation pressure is not a healthy outlet for labour; if it is Government-aided, helpless, thriftless folk flock to it for a while, and starve on the other side; if land is given, capital is wanted by the emigrant, for before he can eat his own bread, he must clear his land of timber, plough or dig it, sow his corn, and wait for his harvest; if he goes out poor, on what is he to live during the first year? Men with £300 or £400 of capital may find more profitable investment for it in the West in America, or in our colonies, than at home, but their outgoing will not much relieve the labour market. Emigration for penniless agricultural labourers, and for artizans, means only starvation abroad instead of at home. And it is starvation under worse conditions than they had left in the mother-country; they have to face vicissitudes of climate for which they are utterly unprepared, extremes of heat and of cold which try even vigorous constitutions, and simply kill off underfed, half clothed, and ill housed new comers. Nor is work always to be had in the New World. No better proof of the foolishness of emigration to the United States can be given, than the fact that, at the present time, contractors in England are in treaty with American workmen, with the object of bringing them over here. Unskilled labour does not improve its chances by going abroad. Nor is skilled labour in a better position, for here the German emigrant undersells the British; he can live harder and cheaper, and has had a better technical education than has fallen to the lot of his British rival. One great evil connected with emigration is the disproportion it causes between men and women, both in the old country and in the new, those who emigrate being chiefly males. Nor must it be forgotten that when England colonized most, her population was far smaller than it is at the present time; physical vigour is necessary for successful colonizing, and the physical vigour of our labouring poor deteriorates under their present conditions; as the Canadian roughly said at the meeting of the British Association at Plymouth: "the colonies don't want the children of your rickety paupers." Colonization needs the pick of a nation, if it is to succeed, not the poor who are driven from home in search of the necessaries of life. John Stuart Mill points out how inadequate emigration is as a continued relief to population, useful as it is as a sudden effort to lighten pressure; he remarks that the great distance of the fields of emigration prevents them from being a sufficient outlet for surplus labourers; "it still remains to be shown by experience," he says, "whether a permanent stream of emigration can be kept up sufficient to take off, as in America, all that portion of the annual increase (when proceeding at its greatest rapidity) which, being in excess of the progress made during the same short period in the arts of life, tends to render living more difficult for every averagely situated individual in the community. And unless this can be done, emigration cannot, even in an economical point of view, dispense with the necessity of checks to population." 1173 infants are born in the United Kingdom every day, and to equalize matters about 1000 emigrants should leave our shores daily. Careful calculations are sometimes entered into by anti-Malthusians as to the acreage of Great Britain as compared with its population, and it is said that the land would support many more than the present number of inhabitants; quite so; there is a very large quantity of land used for deer, game, and pleasure, that, if put under cultivation, would enormously increase the food-supply. But to know this, does not remedy the pressing evils of over-population; what service is it to the family crowded into a St. Giles' cellar to tell them that there are large uninhabited tracts of land in Pertshire? In the first place they can't get to them, and if they could, they would be taken up for trespassing. Such information is but mockery. Land reform is sorely needed, but, to meet the immediate needs of the present, land revolution would be necessary; it is surely wiser to lessen the population-pressure, and to work steadily at the same time towards Reform of the Land Laws, instead of allowing the population pressure to increase, until the starving multitudes precipitate us into a revolution.

An extraordinary confusion exists in some minds between preventive checks and infanticide. People speak as though prevention were the same as destruction. But no life is destroyed by the prevention of conception, any more than by abstention from marriage ; if it is infanticide for every man and woman not to produce as many children as possible during the fertile period of life, if every person in a state of celibacy commits infanticide because of the potential life he prevents, then, of course, the prevention of conception by married persons is also infanticide ; the two things are on exactly the same level. When conception has taken place, then prevention is no longer possible and a new life having been made, the destruction of that life would be criminal. Before conception no life exists to be destroyed; the seminal fluid is simply a secretion of the body; its fertilizing power is not a living thing, the non-use of which destroys life; the spermatozoa, the active fertilizing agents, are not living existences, and "they have been erroneously considered as proper animalculæ" (Carpenter). Life is not made until the male and female elements are united, and if this is prevented, either by abstention from intercourse among the unmarried, or by preventive intercourse among the married, life is not destroyed, because the life is not yet in existence.

Mr. Darwin puts forward an argument against scientific checks which must not be omitted here; he says:—"The enhancement of the welfare of mankind is a most intricate problem ; all ought to refrain from marriage who cannot avoid abject poverty for their children, for poverty is not only a great evil, but tends to its own increase by leading to recklessness in marriage. On the other hand, as Mr. Galton has remarked, if the prudent avoid marriage, whilst the reckless marry, the inferior members tend to supplant the better members of society. Man, like every other animal, has no doubt advanced to his present high condition through a struggle for existence, consequent on his rapid multiplication, and if he is to advance still higher it is to be feared that he must remain subject to a severe struggle ; otherwise he would sink into indolence, and the more gifted men would not be more successful in the battle of life than the less gifted. Hence our natural rate of increase, though leading to many and obvious evils, must not be greatly diminished by any means."

If the struggle for existence among mankind were waged under the same conditions as among animals, then Mr.

Darwin's argument would have great force, terrible as would be the amount of human misery caused by it. Then the strongest, cleverest, craftiest, would survive, and would transmit their qualities to their offspring. But Mr. Darwin forgets that men have qualities which the brutes have not, such as compassion, justice, respect for the right of others —and all these, man's highest virtues, are absolutely incompatible with the brutal struggle for existence. Where the lion would leave his parents to starve, man would feed his; where the stag would kill the sickly one, man would carry him to the hospital and nurse him back to health. The feeble, the deformed, the helpless, are killed out in brute nature; in human nature they are guarded, tended, nourished, and they hand on to their offspring their own disabilities. Scientific checks to population would just do for man what the struggle for existence does for the brutes: they enable man to control the production of new human beings; those who suffer from hereditary diseases, who have consumption or insanity in the family, might marry, if they so wished, but would preserve the race from the deterioration which results from propagating disease. The whole British race would gain in vigour, in health, in longevity, in beauty, if only healthy parents gave birth to children; at present there is many a sickly family, because sickly persons marry; they revolt against forbiddance of marriage, celibacy being unnatural, and they are taught that "the natural consequences of marriage" must follow. Let them understand that one set of "consequences" results naturally from one set of conditions, another set from different conditions, and let them know that *laisser aller* in marriage is no wiser than in other paths of life.

Leaving objectors, let us look at the other side of the question. The system of preventive checks to population points us to the true pathway of safety; it is an immediate relief, and at once lightens the burden of poverty. Each married couple have it in their power to avoid poverty for themselves and for their children, by determining, when they enter on married life, that they will not produce a family larger than they can comfortably maintain: thus they avoid the daily harass of domestic struggle; they rejoice over two healthy, robust, well fed children, instead of mourning over seven frail, sickly, half starved ones; they look forward to an old age of comfort and of respectability instead of one of painful dependence on a grudgingly-given charity.

How rapidly conjugal prudence may lift a nation out of

pauperism is seen in France; the proportion of adults to the whole population is the largest in Europe, the proportionate number of persons under thirty being the smallest; hence, there are more producers and fewer non-producers than in any other country. The consequence of this is that the producers are less pressed upon, and live in greater comfort and with more enjoyment of life. There are no less than 5,000,000 of properties under six acres, each sufficient to support a small family, but wholly inadequate for the maintenance of a large one, and it was from these independent peasants that M. Thiers borrowed the money to pay off the indemnity levied by the Germans after the late war. If those peasants had been struggling under the difficulties of large families, no savings would have been made to fall back upon in such an emergency. France shows a pattern of widely-spread comfort which we look for in vain in our own land, and this comfort is directly traceable to the systematic regard for conjugal prudence. Small agricultural holdings directly tend to this virtue, the fact of the limitation of the food-supply available being obvious to the most ignorant peasant. So strongly rooted is this habit in France, that the Roman Church in vain branded it as a deadly sin, and Dr. Drysdale writes that a French priest begged the Vatican Council to change this direction; he said, "It is not the sin which is new, but the circumstances which have changed. This practice has been spreading more and more for half a century from the force of things. As Providence does not multiply animals, when they have not wherewithal to eat, so it will not require reasonable man voluntarily to multiply when there is no longer the condition for his subsistence. This is human calculation, pecuniary motives if you will, but a calculation as inevitable as destiny. Countries enjoying the faith do not thus calculate, it is true, and so long as obedience is possible they will obey the priest without a murmur; but a day will come when the prevailing doctrine will be applicable to them all, and hence we earnestly plead for reform. Other times, other customs. The laws should change with the customs."

It is well worthy of notice that those who have pleaded for scientific checks to population, have also been those who have been identified with the struggle for political and religious freedom; Carlile defended the use of such—as advocated in his " Every Woman's Book "—as follows:—

" There are four grounds on which my ' Every Woman's Book ' and its recommendation can be defended, and each of them in itself sufficient to justify the publication, and to make it meritorious. First—the political or national ground, which refers to the strength and wealth of the nation, and the greatest happiness of the greatest number of the people. Second—the local or commercial ground, or the ground of the wages of labour, and its supply in the several trades and districts. Third—the domestic or family ground, where the parents may think they have already children enough, and that more will be an injury. Fourth—the individual ground, where the state of health in the female, or her situation in life, will not justify a pregnancy; but where the abstinence from love becomes as great an evil. It has been a sort of common, but ill-judged maxim, that the strength and wealth of a nation consist in the number, the greatest number, of its people. The error in the judgment of the maxim is, in not taking into consideration whether that number be well or ill employed, well or ill fed, clothed and housed. If the number be well employed, well fed, well clothed, well housed, then the greatness of the number is in reality the wealth and strength of the nation. But if, on the other hand, the greatness of the number lessens the means of good employment, good living, clothing and housing, then, as in England and Ireland, at this moment, under the present arrangements of government, aristocracy, religion, &c., the greatness of the number constitutes the weakness of the nation; and England and Ireland are both weak at this moment: weak, too evidently weak, from ill employed or unemployed members of the people. It is objected to me, that there is a sufficiency of natural checks already in existence, to remedy the evils of which I complain. My answer is, that these natural checks are the evil of which I do complain, and *which I seek to remove by the substitution of a* MORAL CHECK, *that shall furnish no pain, no degradation no discomfort, no evil of any kind.* The existing natural or physical checks are disease or pestilence and famine. Surely it is to be desired that neither of these should exist. It is not wise, not parental, not kind, to breed children to such disasters. It is better that they should not be born, than be cut off prematurely by disease or famine, or struggle through a life of disease, poverty, and misery, a life of pain to themselves, and both a pain and burthen to their parents. The existing moral checks on numbers are war, and social arrangements, such as poverty, late marriages, celibacy, and the bad health which bad states of living produce; to which may be added, states of servitude, in which marriage is found inconvenient. These are all so many evils—all will say. It would be well to go on without war, and the time will come when wars will cease. In the question of trade, a government can do nothing more than remove impediments. It cannot increase the amount of trade beyond its natural demand. It cannot force trade to any permanent utility. Therefore I take it to be a clear point, that no change in government will do anything permanently for the relief of the present number of persons employed in surplus production. In limiting the number of children, as applicable to such a case, there is a double relief; an immediate relief to the parents, in not incurring expenses which cannot be well met, and a remote relief, in not bringing forth new labourers, when those existing cannot find employment. Besides, there is something cruel, wanton, base, and parentally unfeeling, in the principle that says: 'I will bring all the children I can into the world, and if I cannot maintain them some other persons who care nothing about them must, or, which is the real alternative, they may starve.'"

Mr. Francis Place argues: "The mass of the people in an old country must remain in a state of wretchedness, until they are convinced that their safety depends upon themselves, and that it can be maintained in no other way than by their ceasing to propagate faster than the means of comfortable subsistence are produced. . . . .

"If above all it were once clearly understood that it was not disreputable for married persons to avail themselves of such precautionary means as would, without being injurious to health or destructive of female delicacy, *prevent conception*, a sufficient check might at once be given to the increase of population beyond the means of subsistence, and vice and misery to a prodigious extent might be removed from society. . . . . If means were adopted to prevent the breeding of a larger number of children than married people might desire to have, and if the labouring part of the population could thus be kept below the demand for labour, wages would rise, so as to afford the means of comfortable subsistence for all, and all might marry. . . . .

"It is time that those who really understand the cause of a redundant, unhappy, miserable, and considerably vicious population, and the means of preventing the redundancy, should clearly, freely, openly, and fearlessly point out the means."

Mr. James Watson showed his view of the matter by publishing Dr. Charles Knowlton's " Fruits of Philosophy."

Mr. Robert Dale Owen (son of Robert Owen, and American minister in Florence), in his " Moral Physiology," urges " some 'moral restraint' that shall not, like vice and misery, be demoralizing, nor, like late marriages, be ascetic and impracticable;" and he proceeds to advocate and describe scientific checks.

Mr. James Mill complains that the problem of checking population is "miserably evaded by all those who have meddled with the subject;" and says that " if the superstitions of the nursery were disregarded, and the principle of utility kept steadily in view, a solution might not be very difficult to be found."

Mr. John Stuart Mill strongly urges restraint of the number of the family, and he took an active part in disseminating the knowledge of scientific checks.

The members of the old Freethought Institution in John Street made it part of their work to circulate popular tracts, advocating scientific checks, such as a four-page tract entitled, " Population : is not its increase at present an evil, and would not some harmless check be desirable?"

Mr. Austin Holyoake, in his " Large and Small Families," follows in the same strain, and recommends as guides Knowlton's Pamphlet and Owen's " Moral Physiology."

Mr. George Jacob Holyoake, writing as one of the Vice-Presidents of the National Secular Society in 1876, points to the difference between Christian and Secular morality on this head ; he says : " Let any one regard for a moment the Christian's theory of this life. It tells us that all human beings born are immortal, and that God has to provide for them above or below! Yet in every portion of the land scoundrel or vicious parents may bring into existence a squalid brood of dirty, sickly, depraved, ignorant, ragged children. Christianity fails utterly to prevent their existence, and hurls quick words of opprobrium upon any who advocate the prevention of this progeny of crime. Yet the Christian teaches that, by mere act of orthodox belief, these ignorant and unclean creatures can be sent from the gutter to God. A Secularist cannot help shuddering at this doctrine and this practice, so fatal to society, so contemptuous to heaven."

M. Garnier—and with him I close these extracts, only a few out of many that might be brought forward—says: " I am led to declare openly and positively, that by pru-

A DISCUSSION
—— OF THE ——
SOCIAL QUESTION
—— BETWEEN ——
Juliet H. Severance, M. D., and David Jones.

"So far as I know, Juliet H. Severance's words are not misunderstood. Her 'Discussion of the Social Question' was the first defense of the liberty of woman in the marriage relation that I ever read — that is, the first that left a lasting impression. I first read an extract, then got the book and was oblivious to all else until I had read every word. I shall never forget that experience. The language so vivid, the arguments so unanswerable, the style so terse, *so plain* — carried with them a conviction that has never been shaken — that never can be shaken, I firmly believe. I thank Juliet H. Severance for that work. It has greatly benefited me. It has helped many other women, and will help many more in the years to come."

OCTAVO. 53 PAGES. PRICE, 15 CENTS.

THE
TRIAL OF THE JUDGMENT.
A REVIEW OF THE
ANARCHIST CASE.
By GENERAL M. M. TRUMBULL,

Author of "The American Lesson of the Free-Trade Struggle in England, and "Was it a Fair Trial?"

Seventy-five Octavo Pages.   Price, 25 cts.

THE PRODIGAL DAUGHTER,
—OR, THE—
PRICE OF VIRTUE.
By RACHEL CAMPBELL.

This is one of the bravest, as well as entertaining and useful, pamphlets published. It has been aptly called "The GREATEST *little* book of the Century." It is having an extensive sale. New edition just out. Price, 10cts.

Address, FAIR PLAY, *Valley Falls, Kansas.*

dence is to be understood not only delayed marriages, not only celibacy for those who are capable of practicing it, but prudence during the married state itself." Answering Proudhon's objections, he asks : " Can it be called immoral in the father of a family if he should wish to have only a limited number of children, proportioned to his means, and to the future which his affection fondly weaves for them, and if he should not, in carrying out this object, condemn himself to the most absolute and rigorous continence ?..... Let any one ask himself whether it is more moral, more conscientious, to give birth to children in the midst of privations, or prevent them being born, and let him then reply."

Thus has the effort to obtain social reform gone hand in hand with that for political and religious freedom ; the victors in the latter have been the soldiers in the former. Discussion on the Population Question is not yet safe; legal penalty threatens those who advocate the restriction of birth instead of the destruction of life; the same penalty was braved by our leaders in the last generation, and we have only to follow in their steps in order to conquer as they conquered and become sharers of their crown. We work for the redemption of the poor, for the salvation of the wretched; the cause of the people is the sacredest of all causes, and is the one which is the most certain to triumph, however sharp may be the struggle for the victory.

THE END.